Big or Not?

LEVEL 1

/b/

DECODABLES

BY jump!

Teaching Tips

Pink Level 1

This book focuses on the phoneme **/b/**.

Before Reading

- Discuss the title. Ask readers what they think the book will be about.
- Sound out the words on page 3 together.

Read the Book

- Ask readers to use a finger to follow along with each word as it is read.
- Encourage readers to break down unfamiliar words into units of sound. Then, ask them to string the sounds together to create the words.
- Urge readers to point out when the focused phonics phoneme appears in the text.

After Reading

- Encourage children to reread the book independently or with a friend.
- Ask simple questions about the text to check for understanding. Have them find the pages that have the answers to your questions.

5357 Penn Avenue South
Minneapolis, MN 55419
www.jumplibrary.com

Decodables by Jump! are published by Jump! Library.

Library of Congress Cataloging-in-Publication Data is available at www.loc.gov or upon request from the publisher.

ISBN: 979-8-88996-762-0 (hardcover)
ISBN: 979-8-88996-763-7 (paperback)
ISBN: 979-8-88996-764-4 (ebook)

Photo Credits
Images are courtesy of Shutterstock.com. With thanks to Getty Images, Thinkstock Photo and iStockphoto. Cover – Donovan van Staden, Rudmer Zwerver. 4–5 – Eric Isselee, Erik Lam. 6–7 – Alex Staroseltsev, djgis. 8–9 – LOGVINYUK YULIIA, Trendsetter Images. 10–11 – Philip Lange, S.Borisov. 14–15 – Shutterstock.

Can you find these words in the book?

big

bug

Is it big?

It is not.

Is the bug big?

It is not.

Is it big?

It is not.

Is it big?

It is! Big Ben is big.

Can you say this sound and draw it with your finger?

Can you say this word and draw it with your finger?

big

What other words do you know that start with the letter /b/?

Practice reading the book again:

Is it big?

It is not.

Is the bug big?

It is not.

Is it big?

It is not.

Is it big?

It is! Big Ben is big.